The Battle at the McGoverns'

A STORY ABOUT FAMILY ARGUMENTS

Written by
JOY BERRY

WORD INC.
Waco, Texas 76796

About the Author and Publisher

Joy Berry's mission in life is to help families cope with everyday problems and to help children become competent, responsible, happy individuals. To achieve her goal, she has written over two hundred self-help books for children from infancy through age twelve. Her work has revolutionized children's publishing by providing families with practical, how-to, living skills information that was previously unavailable in children's books.

Joy has gathered a dedicated team of experts, including psychologists, educators, child developmentalists, writers, editors, designers, and artists to form her publishing company and to help produce her work.

The company, Living Skills Press, produces thoroughly researched books and audiovisual materials that successfully combine humor and education to teach children subjects ranging from how to clean a bedroom to how to resolve problems and get along with other people.

Copyright © 1987 by Joy Berry
Living Skills Press, Sebastopol, CA
All rights reserved.
Printed in the United States of America.

Managing Editor: Ellen Klarberg
Copy Editor: Annette Gooch
Editorial Assistant: Lana Eberhard

Art Director: Laurie Westdahl
Assistant Art Director: Caroline Rennard
Designer: Laurie Westdahl
Production: Margaret Parks, Caroline Rennard
Illustration Design: Bartholomew
Inker: Linda Hanney
Colorer: Linda Hanney
Composition: TBH/Typecast, Inc.
Published by Word Incorporated
in cooperation with Living Skills Press

Hello, my name is Joy, and I'd like to tell you a story about Maggie and some valuable lessons she learned about families and family arguments.

It was a tie score in the last inning with two outs and a runner on third. Jennifer Westley was her little league team's last hope.

"It's up to you, Jennifer," Maggie said somberly as her teammate picked up a bat and walked toward the batter's box.

Everyone on and off the field watched anxiously as the pitcher wound up. The ball came racing toward Jennifer, and she swung.

There was a sharp crack as the bat connected and sent the ball into orbit. It sailed to left field and clear out of the park.

Jennifer loped easily around the bases, and the entire team met her in front of the dugout.

"All right! Way to go!" Maggie congratulated her.

When the excitement of the game had worn off, the two girls helped load the equipment into the coach's car.

"Hey, Maggie, how about spending the night at my house sometime?" Jennifer said.

Maggie's heart went into high gear. There was no kid she admired more than Jennifer.

"Of course I want to spend the night!" she thought to herself. "But if I do, Jennifer will expect me to invite her to my house, and . . ."

Maggie's train of thought was interrupted by Jennifer's voice. "Did you hear what I said?"

"Yeah, I heard what you said. When do you want me to come?" Maggie blurted out.

"How about coming over next Saturday after the game?" Jennifer asked.

It was too late for Maggie to back out now. "Sure! I'll come over," Maggie said.

At home, Maggie told her mother about Jennifer's invitation. "It was nice of Jennifer to invite you to her house," Mrs. McGovern said. "You'll have to return the favor. How about having her come over the week-end after you go to her house?"

"Jennifer? Come to our house?" Maggie asked nervously.

"Of course! It might not be good enough for the Queen of England, but I think that our house is quite sufficient for Jennifer!" Mrs. McGovern said, trying to be humorous.

But Maggie wasn't laughing. The idea of Jennifer being in the McGovern house amidst its chaos and clutter put a sick feeling in the pit of Maggie's stomach.

Jennifer Westley was an only child and a straight-A student whose all-American beauty was surpassed only by her musical talents and athletic ability. She appeared to be flawless in every way, and Maggie was certain that she came from a disgustingly perfect family.

The sleep-over at Jennifer's house confirmed Maggie's suspicions. After the game, Mrs. Westley was waiting for the girls in a brand new station wagon.

"Gosh!" Maggie thought to herself. "She looks more like a model than a mother."

Shortly after the two girls walked into the impeccably clean house, Maggie met the father who completed the picture-perfect family.

Just as Maggie expected, everything about Jennifer's situation was not to be believed. There was not a single mess anywhere. The toilet paper rolls were full instead of empty. Dry towels were neatly hanging by the tub and shower, and the refrigerator was not stuffed with several weeks of moldy leftovers. But more important, it was totally peaceful, and there was not a single argument.

"This is heaven!" Maggie thought as she sat down to a dinner that consisted of some of her favorite foods.

"Have you ever thought of adopting a sister for Jennifer?" Maggie said jokingly.

Jennifer's mother responded good-naturedly, "No, not really."

"Well, if you ever change your mind, I'd like to apply for the position!" Maggie said with a giggle, and everyone laughed.

That night, as Maggie lay between the clean sheets on the bed next to Jennifer's, she began to worry about inviting her special friend to spend the night at her house.

"The poor kid would never survive the experience!" Maggie reasoned. "She's used to having her own bedroom, her own bathroom, and her own TV. She never had to fight for her turn to use anything!"

Just then, Jennifer spoke softly, "Good night, Maggie. I'm glad you came over."

"I'm glad I came over, too!" Maggie said.

And with that, both girls snuggled into their beds and fell asleep.

The next week was pure torture for Maggie. She was torn between the desire to spend time with Jennifer and the desire to avoid her. Jennifer was waiting for an invitation, and Maggie knew it. When Friday came, Maggie had to face the fact that it was time for her to make a move. With sweaty palms and butterflies in her stomach, she approached Jennifer after baseball practice.

"I realize this is pretty late notice, and you'll probably have to say no, but I thought I'd ask you anyway. Would you like to sleep over at my house tomorrow night?"

"I'd love to!" Jennifer shrieked with delight. "I'll bring all my stuff to the game and then . . ."

Maggie frantically interrupted, "Well. . . well, don't you have to talk to your parents before we make final plans?"

"I already talked to them!" Jennifer beamed. "I had a hunch you'd invite me so I got permission ahead of time."

"Oh, really? That's neat," Maggie said unconvincingly.

The next morning, Maggie was up at the crack of dawn. She made a list of everything that needed to be done before Jennifer's arrival. Number one on her list was a top-to-bottom cleaning of the bedroom she shared with her baby sister, and number two was a general clean-up of the common living areas in the house. The list also included begging her brothers to get their rooms into a presentable state. Maggie successfully completed the first task on her list and, with her mother's unflagging assistance, the second goal was accomplished.

But the boys' bedrooms were a different matter. Maggie knew that nothing short of a death threat or a million dollar bribe could motivate her brothers into action when it came to cleaning their rooms. So she decided to resort to keeping their bedroom doors closed. That way, Jennifer wouldn't see what could easily be mistaken for the city dump.

Jennifer's visit was going more smoothly than Maggie thought it would. Luckily, Jennifer didn't seem to notice the fingerprint smudges on the walls or the dirty stains on the heavily used furniture and carpets. And luckily, she didn't seem to notice that Maggie walked several paces ahead, closing the doors to various rooms before Jennifer could see inside them.

Dinnertime at the McGoverns' was far more loud and raucous than it had been at the Westleys'. Even so, Maggie was thankful because the usual disagreements over food and attention were quickly resolved before they had a chance to become knock-down-drag-out fights.

"It's almost over," a relieved Maggie thought to herself as she and Jennifer sat down to watch television.

Unfortunately, Maggie's feelings of relief were premature.

Just then, one of Maggie's brothers came into the room and walked over to the television set.

"This is just a stupid rerun," he said glibly as he proceeded to change the channel.

"Get your grubby hands off of that knob!" another brother said as he entered the family room. "I stayed home tonight just so I could watch the football game."

Sam, Maggie's youngest brother, quickly joined the feuding siblings.

"Neither of you gets to decide what we're going to watch on TV," he asserted.

By this time, the two older brothers were in each other's face and totally oblivious to anything Sam had to say.

Realizing that he was being ignored, a frustrated Sam began to scream at the top of his lungs, "Mom! Mom! They won't let me choose the TV program!"

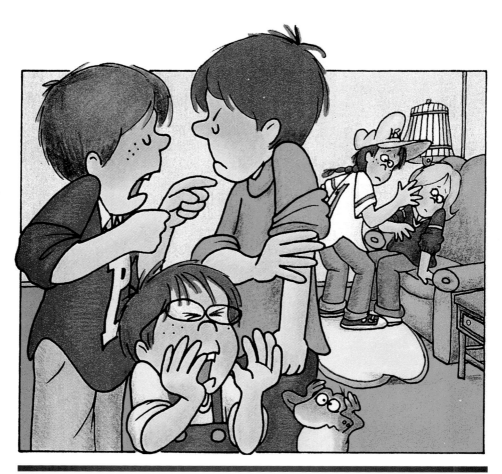

Seeing that the argument between the boys was thirty seconds away from turning into a total disaster, Maggie grabbed Jennifer by the arm and began to drag her out of the family room. Jennifer was confused.

"What are you doing?" Jennifer stammered.

"I'm getting you away from a situation that could possibly endanger your life!" Maggie said sarcastically.

Once the two girls were inside Maggie's bedroom, Maggie slammed the door behind them. By this time, almost every family member was involved in the argument over the TV. And even with the bedroom door closed, the girls could still hear the bickering.

Maggie was so mortified she found it impossible to look Jennifer in the eyes. So she flopped herself down on her bed and stared at the ceiling.

"Look, Jennifer," she began, "what can I say? I really hoped that . . ."

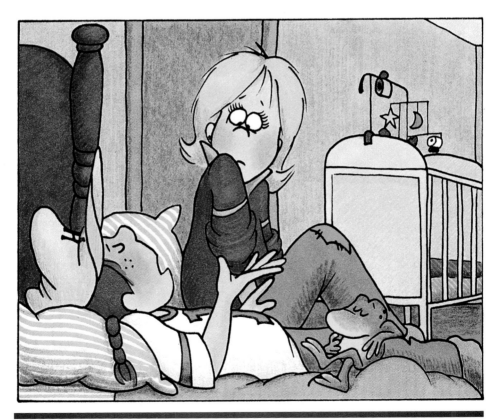

Before Maggie could finish her sentence, Jennifer burst out laughing.

Maggie sat straight up and looked with disbelief at Jennifer who was doubled over with laughter.

"What's so funny?" Maggie demanded.

Jennifer calmed down long enough to say, "The entire situation!"

"Are you laughing at my family?" Maggie asked defensively.

"Of course not!" Jennifer replied. "I'm laughing at me and *my* family!"

Jennifer's response only added to Maggie's confusion. "What do you mean?" Maggie questioned.

Jennifer began, "If you could see our family when no one is around . . . we fight like cats and dogs!"

A stunned look told Jennifer that Maggie was having a hard time believing what she was hearing.

Jennifer continued, "You don't know what it's like to live with a mom who prides herself in having floors that are clean enough to eat off of. I always say who cares? Nobody's going to be eating off the floors!"

Maggie chuckled, and Jennifer kept talking.

"And you don't know what it's like to have a dad who's constantly saying things like, 'You've gotta work, work, work if you want to get ahead.' I say I'd rather stay behind and have more fun! I tell you, Maggie, seeing your family argue does my heart good. It makes me think that maybe family arguments aren't so bad. Maybe they're a part of family life!"

Maggie began to relax. For the first time, Jennifer was beginning to sound like a normal kid.

Maggie jumped to her feet and spoke up. "Well, if you're used to family arguments, what do you think about going back to the family room? I think *we've* got a pretty good case for being the ones to choose the TV program. After all, we were the ones who turned on the TV!"

The mischievous twinkle in Jennifer's eye said that she was game. "I say let's go for it!" she said excitedly.

And with that, the two determined girls headed back
to the war zone.

Of course, both Maggie and Jennifer realized that they might not win the battle, but one thing was for sure . . . they'd have a lot of fun trying!

So what can we learn from all of this?

Maggie learned that situations can sometimes appear to be perfect when in reality they aren't. This is especially true of family situations.

There is no such thing as a perfect family situation. Every family, no matter how large or how small, has conflicts and problems that can result in family arguments.

Family arguments are normal and can be a positive part of family life if they are handled appropriately.

It is *not* appropriate for family members to
- hurt each other physically,
- purposely hurt each other's feelings, or
- damage or destroy things.

To handle arguments appropriately, family members need to

- take time to think about the situation,
- calmly talk about it, and
- do whatever is necessary to resolve the conflict in a way that is fair to everyone who is involved.

Family arguments can be helpful if
- family members are allowed to say what is upsetting them,
- problems are dealt with and resolved, or
- family members learn valuable lessons.

EPILOGUE

Pamela and I went to Maggie's house the other day to work on a Human Race Club project. We had a pretty hard time finding an uncluttered place to work. I got a kick out of what Maggie told us.

"You'd never find clutter like this at Jennifer's house," she said with a chuckle. "But then again, according to Jennifer, you wouldn't have as much fun at her house either."